THE
Quick
JOB
SEARCH

J. MICHAEL FARR

JIST Works, Inc.
The Job Search People
720 North Park Avenue
Indianapolis, IN 46202

About the Author

Mike Farr has authored a variety of books on job seeking skills that have sold over 400,000 copies. He specializes in techniques that get results and has trained thousands of instructors to teach more effective job seeking skills. Other books by the author include:

Job Finding Fast. A most thorough text-workbook providing substantial information and activities in the areas of self-exploration, career decision making and job seeking. $10.95

Getting The Job You Really Want. A text-workbook covering the same topics as *Job Finding Fast* in a shorter, easy-to-read format. Also contains information on job survival and success. $8.25

The Work Book. A standard feature of many results-oriented job search programs. Over 300,000 sold. $9.95

The JIST Job Search Course: A Young Person's Guide To Getting And Keeping A Good Job. A job search text-workbook

The publisher provides a free catalog containing over 600 items of career and job search materials to qualified institutions and instructors. Quantity prices for *The Quick Job Search* are also available, as are instructor's guides for the books listed above.

Production Supervisor: Ruth Lister
Editor: Carole Black
Cover/Interior Design: Ron Troxell
Calligraphy: Debb Hibbs

JIST Works, Inc.
720 North Park Avenue
Indianapolis, IN 46202
317/264/3720 • 800/648/JIST • FAX 317/264/3709

ISBN: 0-942784-21-9

The Quick Job Search

How to Make Your Job Search Quick

It's not easy finding a job. But research has proven that by using the right methods, most people can reduce the time it takes to find one. They also tend to earn a little more and be a little more satisfied with the jobs they find. So can you.

This book is designed to cover the basics of looking for work. The topics it covers are based on sound research and many years of experience. It covers the job search techniques that work best and reduce the time it takes to get a job.

There is, of course, much more you can learn about looking for a job. There are many books on the subject, and some are better than others. Other books by the author are listed at the front of the book.

But don't just *read* about looking for a job. The best way to get a job is to *go out there and get interviews!* And the best way to get interviews is to *make a job out of getting a job.* That's what this book will help you do.

Here are the six basic steps of a quick and successful job search:

1. Know your skills.
2. Have a clear job objective.
3. Know where and how to look.
4. Spend at least 25 hours a week looking.
5. Get two interviews a day.
6. Follow up on all contacts.

Know Your Skills

One survey of employers found that 90% of the people they interviewed could not explain their skills. They could not answer the question "Why should I hire you?"

Knowing what you are good at is very important in interviewing. It also helps you decide what type of job you will enjoy and do well. Most people think of "skills" as job related skills. A secretary, for example needs to type. But everyone has other skills that are very important to success on a job. The two most important are self-management and transferable skills.

Self-Management Skills

Write down three things about yourself that you think make you a good worker.

1. _____
2. _____
3. _____

The things you wrote down may be the most important things for an employer to know about you! They have to do with your basic personality, your ability to manage yourself in a new environment. They are some of the most important things to bring up in an interview. Review the following list and put a checkmark beside any skills you have. After you are done with the list, circle five skills you feel are most important. The first group, Key Skills, are ones that employers find particularly important. If one or more of the Key Skills apply to you, mentioning them in an interview can help you greatly.

Key Skills

____ accept supervision   ____ hard worker
____ get along with co-workers ____ honest
____ get things done on time   ____ punctual
____ good attendance   ____ productive

Other Skills

____ ambitious   ____ mature
____ assertive   ____ methodical
____ capable   ____ modest
____ cheerful   ____ motivated
____ competent   ____ natural

___ completes assignments
___ conscientious
___ able to coordinate
___ creative
___ dependable
___ discreet
___ eager
___ efficient
___ energetic
___ enthusiastic
___ expressive
___ flexible
___ formal
___ friendly
___ good natured
___ helpful
___ humble
___ imaginative
___ independent
___ industrious
___ informal
___ intelligent
___ intuitive
___ learn quickly
___ loyal

___ open minded
___ optimistic
___ original
___ patient
___ persistent
___ physically strong
___ practice new skills
___ take pride in work
___ reliable
___ resourceful
___ responsible
___ self-confident
___ sense of humor
___ sincere
___ solve problems
___ spontaneous
___ steady
___ tactful
___ tenacious
___ thrifty
___ trustworthy
___ versatile
___ well organized

Other similar skills you have:

_____

_____

_____

Note: Some people find it helpful to complete the section called "Essential Job Search Data" on page 21. Those of you with work experience may find it helpful to use that section to list your skills and accomplishments from previous jobs and other life experiences. Then you will have a better idea what skills you have that you may want to use on your next job.

Transferable Skills

These are skills you can transfer from one job or career to another. Some are more important in one job than another. *Your success requires you to find a job that needs the skills you have.*

Put a check beside the skills in the following list that you have. You may have used them in a previous job or in some non-work setting. When done, circle the five skills you feel are most important to use in your next job.

Key Skills

___ instructing others
___ managing money, budget
___ managing people
___ meeting deadlines
___ meeting the public
___ negotiating
___ organizing/managing projects
___ public speaking
___ written communication skills

Working with Things

___ assemble things
___ build things
___ construct/repair building
___ drive, operate vehicles
___ good with hands
___ observe/inspect
___ operating tools, machines
___ repair things
___ use complex equipment

Working with Data

___ analyze data
___ audit records
___ budgeting
___ calculate/compute
___ check for accuracy
___ classify things
___ compare
___ compile
___ count
___ detail oriented
___ evaluate
___ investigate
___ keep financial records
___ locate answers, information
___ manage money
___ observe/inspect
___ record facts
___ research
___ synthesize
___ take inventory

Working with People

___ advise
___ administer
___ care for
___ confront others
___ counsel people
___ patient
___ perceptive
___ persuade
___ pleasant
___ sensitive

___ demonstrate
___ diplomatic
___ help others
___ instruct
___ interview people
___ kind
___ listen
___ negotiate
___ outgoing

___ sociable
___ supervise
___ tactful
___ teaching
___ tolerant
___ tough
___ trusting
___ understanding

Working with Words, Ideas

___ articulate
___ communicate verbally
___ correspond with others
___ create new ideas
___ design
___ edit
___ ingenious

___ inventive
___ library research
___ logical
___ public speaking
___ remembering information
___ write clearly

Leadership

___ arrange social functions
___ competitive
___ decisive
___ delegate
___ direct others
___ explain things to others
___ influence others
___ initiate new tasks
___ make decisions
___ manage or direct others

___ mediate problems
___ motivate people
___ negotiate agreements
___ planning
___ results oriented
___ risk taker
___ run meetings
___ self-confident
___ self-motivate
___ solve problems

Creative/Artistic

___ artistic
___ drawing, art
___ expressive

___ perform, act
___ present artistic idea
___ dance, body movement

Other similar skills you have:

_____
_____
_____

Job Content Skills

These are the skills you need to do a particular job. A carpenter, for example, needs to know how to use various tools and be familiar with a variety of tasks related to that job. Use the space below to list the special job content skills you have from previous jobs, hobbies, training or other life experiences. Use separate sheets for each group of related job content skills as needed.

_____

_____

_____

_____

_____

_____

Have a Clear Job Objective

Even if you don't have a specific job title, you *must* know the type of things you want to do and you are good at *before* you start your job search. This means defining *the* job rather than *a* job. If you already have a good idea of the type of job you want, answering the following questions will help you define it even more clearly.

Job Objective Questionnaire

What skills do you have that you want to use? Select the top five skills from the previous lists that you enjoy using and want to use in your next job.

1. _____
2. _____
3. _____
4. _____
5. _____

What type of special knowledge do you have that you might use in your next job? Perhaps you know how to fix radios, keep accounting records or cook food. Write down the things you know about from schooling, training, hobbies, family experiences and other sources. Perhaps one or more of them could make you a very special applicant in the right setting.

_____
_____
_____
_____
_____
_____

What type of people do you prefer to work with? Do you prefer to work by yourself, to be part of a group or to supervise others?

_____
_____
_____

What type of work environment do you prefer? Do you want to work inside, outside, in a quiet place, a busy place, a clean place, have a window with a nice view?

_____
_____
_____

Where do you want your next job to be located—what city or region? Near a busline? If you are open to live or work anywhere, what would your ideal community be like?

_____
_____
_____

How much money do you hope to make in your next job? Many people will take less money if the job is great in other ways—or to survive. Think about the minimum you would take as well as what you would eventually like to earn. Your next job will probably be somewhere between.

_____

_____

How much responsibility are you willing to accept? Usually, the more money you want to make, the more responsibility you must accept. Do you want to work by yourself, be part of a group, or be in charge? If so, at what level?

_____

_____

What things are important or have meaning to you that you would prefer to include as a basis of the work you do? For example, some people work to help others, some to clean up our environment, build things, make machines work, gain power or prestige, or care for animals or plants. Think about what is important to you and how you might include this in your next job.

_____

_____

_____

Your Ideal Job

Use the points above to help you define the ideal job for you. Think about each one and select the points that are most important to you. Write them on a separate piece of paper.

If you need help figuring out what type of job to look for, remember that most areas have free or low cost career counseling and testing services. Contact local government agencies and schools for referrals.

Avoid a job title that is too narrow, like "secretary" or "COBOL Programmer." Better objectives might be "General Office/Office Manager" or "Programming/Systems Analysis."

Most libraries have a copy of the *Occupational Outlook Handbook* which gives excellent information on over 200 of the most popular jobs. Reading it will help you keep your options open. Many interesting jobs will need a person with your skills, but have job titles that you may not have considered. When you are clear about what type of job you want, write it in the following spaces.

My Job Objective:

_____

_____

_____

Know Where and How to Look

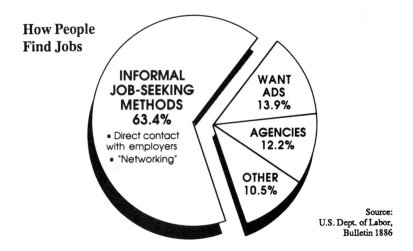

How People Find Jobs

INFORMAL JOB-SEEKING METHODS 63.4%
• Direct contact with employers
• "Networking"

WANT ADS 13.9%

AGENCIES 12.2%

OTHER 10.5%

Source:
U.S. Dept. of Labor,
Bulletin 1886

One survey found that 85% of all employers don't advertise at all. They hire people they already know, who find out about the jobs through word of mouth, or they simply happen to be at the right place at the right time. This is sometimes just luck, but this book will teach you ways to increase your "luck" in finding job openings.

The chart above shows that fewer than 15% of all job seekers get jobs from reading the want ads. Let's take a quick look at want ads and other traditional job search methods.

Traditional Job Search Methods

Help Wanted Ads: Everyone who reads the paper knows about these job openings. So competition for these jobs is fierce. Still, some people do get jobs this way, so go ahead and apply. Just be sure to spend most of your time using more effective methods.

The State Employment Service: Often called the "Unemployment Office," offers free job leads. Only about 5% of all job seekers get their jobs here. This service usually knows of only one-tenth (or fewer)of the available jobs in your area. Still, it is worth a weekly visit. If you ask for the same counselor, you might impress them enough to remember you and refer you to the better openings.

Private Employment Agencies: One out of 20 job seekers get their jobs using a private agency. This means that 95% don't. They charge a fee to either you (as high as 20% of your annual salary!) or the employer. Most of them call employers asking if they have any openings—something you could do yourself. Unless you have skills that are in high demand, you will probably do better on your own. And save money...

Sending Out Resumes: One survey found that you would have to mail more than 500 unsolicited resumes to get one interview! A much better approach is to contact the person who might hire you by phone to set up an interview directly, *then* send a resume. If you insist on sending out unsolicited resumes, do this on weekends—save your "prime time" for more effective job search techniques.

Filling Out Applications: Most applications are used to screen you out. Larger organizations may require them, but remember that your task is to get an interview, not fill out an application. If you do complete them, make them neat, error free, and do not include anything that could get you screened out. If necessary, leave a problem section blank. It can always be explained after you get an offer.

Personnel Departments: Hardly anyone gets hired by someone in a personnel department. Their job is to screen you and refer the "best" applicants to the person who would actually supervise you. You may need to cooperate with them, but it is often better to go directly to the person who is most likely to supervise you even if there is no job opening just now.

Remember that most organizations don't even have a personnel office — only the larger ones!

Informal Job Search Methods

The chart on page 9 shows that two-thirds of all people get their jobs using informal methods. These jobs are often not advertised and are part of the "hidden" job market. How do you find them?

There are two basic informal job search methods: networking with people you know and making direct contacts with an employer. They are both based on the most important job search rule of all:

Don't wait until the job is open!

Most jobs are filled by someone the employer meets before a job is formally "open." So the trick is to meet people who can hire you *before* a job is available! Instead of saying "Do you have any jobs open?," say "I realize you may not have any openings now, but I would still like to talk to you about the possibility of future openings."

Develop a Network of Contacts

One study found that 40% of all people found their jobs through a lead provided by a friend, a relative or an acquaintance. Developing new contacts is called "networking" and here's how it works:

Make lists of people you know. Develop a list of anyone you are friendly with, then make a separate list for all your relatives. These two lists alone often add up to 25 to 100 people or more. Then think of other groups of people with whom you have something in common, like people you used to work with; people who went to your school; people in your social or sports groups; members of your professional association; former employers; members of your religious group. You may not know many of these people personally, but most *will* help you if you ask them.

Contact them in a systematic way. Each of these people is a contact for you. Obviously, some lists and some people on those lists will be more helpful than others, but almost any one of them could help you find a job lead.

Present yourself well. Start with your friends and relatives. Call them up and tell them you are looking for a job and need their help. Be as clear as possible about what you are looking for and what skills and qualifications you have. Look at the sample JIST Card and phone script on pages 14-15 for presentation ideas.

Ask them for leads. It is possible that they will know of a job opening just right for you. If so, get the details and get right on it! More likely, however, they will not, so here are three questions you should ask.

Three Magic Networking Questions

1. *"Do you know of any openings for a person with my skills?"* If the answer is no, then ask:
2. *"Do you know of someone else who might know of such an opening?"* If they do, get that name and ask for another one. If they don't, then ask:
3. *"Do you know of anyone who might know of someone else who might?"* Another way to ask this is, *"Do you know someone who knows lots of people?"* If all else fails, this will usually get you a name.

How Your Network Expands

Contact these referrals and ask them the same questions. For each original contact, you can extend your network of acquaintances by hundreds of people. It will look like the previous chart. Eventually, one of these people will hire you—or refer you to someone who will!

Contact Employers Directly

It takes more courage, but contacting an employer directly is a very effective job search technique. Use the Yellow Pages to identify types of organizations that could use a person with your skills. Then call the organizations listed and ask to speak to the person who is most likely to hire you. There is a sample telephone script on page 15 to give you ideas about what to say.

You can also just walk in and ask to speak to the person in charge. This is particularly effective in small businesses, but it works surprisingly well in larger ones, too. Remember, you want an interview even if there are no openings now. If your timing is inconvenient, ask for a better time to come back for an interview.

Where the Jobs Are

About two-thirds of all new jobs are now created by small businesses. While the largest corporations have reduced the number

Where People Work

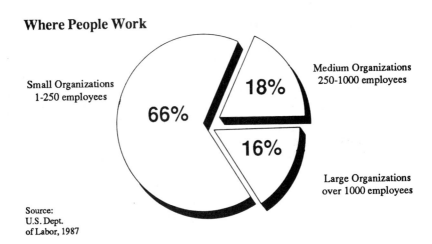

Small Organizations
1-250 employees

66%

Medium Organizations
250-1000 employees

18%

16%

Large Organizations
over 1000 employees

Source:
U.S. Dept.
of Labor, 1987

of employees, small businesses have been creating as many as 80% of the new jobs. There are many opportunities to obtain training and advance in smaller organizations, too. Many do not even have a personnel department, so non-traditional job search techniques are particularly effective with them.

JIST Cards

This is a job search tool that gets results. Typed, printed or even neatly written on a 3" x 5" card, a JIST Card contains the essential information most employers want to know. Look at the sample cards that follow:

Sandy Zaremba

Home: (219) 232-7608   **Message:** (219) 234-7465
Position: General Office/Clerical

Over two years work experience plus one year of training in office practices. Type 55 wpm, trained in word processing operations, post general ledger, handle payables, receivables, and most accounting tasks. Responsible for daily deposits averaging $5,000. Good interpersonal skills. Can meet strict deadlines and handle pressure well.

Willing to work any hours

Organized, honest, reliable, and hard working

THOMAS WELBORN   **Home:** (602) 253-9678
                                       Leave Message: (602) 257-6643

OBJECTIVE: Electronics — installation, maintenance and sales

SKILLS: Four years work experience plus two years advanced training in electronics. A.S. degree in Electronics Engineering Technology. Managed a $300,000/yr. business while going to school full time, with grades in the top 25%. Familiar with all major electronic diagnostic and repair equipment. Hands-on experience with medical, consumer, communications, and industrial electronics equipment and applications. Good problem-solving and communication skills. Customer service oriented.

Willing to do what it takes to get the job done.

JIST Cards are an effective job search tool! Give one to friends and network contacts. Attach it to a resume. Enclose one in your thank you notes before or after an interview. Leave it with employers as a "business card." Use them in many creative ways. Even though they can be typed or even handwritten, it is best to have 100 or more printed so you can put lots of them in circulation. Thousands of job seekers have used them and they get results!

Telephone Contacts

Once you have your JIST Card, it is easy to create a telephone contact "script" based on it. Adapt the basic script to call people you know or your Yellow Pages leads. Just pick out Yellow Page index categories that might use a person with your skills. Then ask for the person who is most likely to supervise you and present your phone script.

While it doesn't work all the time, with practice, most people can get one or more interviews in an hour by making these "cold" calls. Here is a phone script based on another JIST card:

> "Hello, my name is Pam Nykanen. I am interested in a position in hotel management. I have four years experience in sales, catering and accounting with a 300 room hotel. I also have an Associate Degree in Hotel Management plus one year with the Bradey Culinary Institute. During my employment, I helped double revenue from meetings and conferences and increase bar revenues by 46%. I have good problem solving skills and am good with people. I am also well organized, hard working and detail oriented. When can I come in for an interview?"

Spend At Least Twenty-Five Hours a Week

Average job seekers spends about five hours weekly actually looking for work. They are also unemployed an average of three or more months! People who follow JIST's advice spend much more time on their job search each week. They also get jobs in less than half the average time. Time management is the key.

Decide how many hours per week you plan to look for a job. JIST suggests at least 25 hours per week if you are unemployed and are looking for a full time job. The most important thing is to decide how many hours you can commit to your job search and stay with it.

Decide on which days you will look for work. How many hours will you look each day? At what time you will begin and end your job search on each of these days? Look at the sample job search schedule that follows to see how one person planned her time. Create your own schedule on a sheet of paper or, better yet, buy a weekly or monthly planner at a department store or stationery store.

Days	Job Search Schedule	No. of Hours
Monday	8am – Noon, 1-4pm	7
Tuesday	8am – Noon	4
Wednesday	8am – Noon, 1-4 pm	7
Thursday	8am – Noon	4
Friday	8am – 11 am	3
Saturday		
Sunday		
	Total Hours per Week	25

Schedule how to spend your time each day. This is *very* important since most job seekers find it hard to stay productive each day. You already know which job search methods are most effective and you should plan on spending more of your time using these methods. The sample daily schedule that follows has been very effective for people who have used it, and will give you ideas for your own schedule.

Sample Daily Schedule

7:00—8:00 a.m.	Get up, shower, dress, eat breakfast
8:00—8:15	Organize work space; review schedule for interviews or follow ups; update schedule
8:15—9:00	Review old leads for follow up; develop new leads (want ads, Yellow Pages, networking lists, etc.
9:00—10:00	Make phone calls, set up interviews
10:00—10:15	Take a break!
10:15—11:00	Make more calls
11:00—12:00 p.m.	Make follow up calls as needed
12:00—1:00	Lunch break
1:00—5:00	Go on interviews; cold contacts in the field; research for interviews at the library

Get Two Interviews a Day

The average job seeker gets about five interviews a month, fewer than two interviews a week. Yet many job seekers using JIST techniques find it easy to get two interviews a day! To do this, you must re-define what an interview is.

An interview is face to face contact with anyone who has the authority to hire or supervise a person with your skills. They may or may not have a job opening at the time you interview with them.

With this definition, it is *much* easier to get interviews. You can now interview with all kinds of potential employers, not just those who have a job opening. Many job seekers use the Yellow Pages to get two interviews with just an hour of calls by using the telephone contact script discussed earlier! Others simply drop in on potential employers and ask for an unscheduled interview—and they get them. Not always, of course, but often enough.

Getting two interviews a day equals 10 a week—over 40 a month. That's 800% more interviews than the average job seeker gets. Who do you think will get a job offer quicker?

Answering Interview Questions

Here's a list of 10 questions asked most often during interviews:

1. Why don't you tell me about yourself?
2. Why should I hire you?
3. What are your major strengths?
4. What are your major weaknesses?
5. What sort of pay do you expect to receive?
6. How does your previous experience relate to the jobs we have here?
7. What are your plans for the future?
8. What will your former employer (or references) say about you?
9. Why are you looking for this type of position and why here?
10. Why don't you tell me about your personal situation?

We don't have the space here to give thorough answers to all of these questions. There are potentially hundreds more. While the employer may ask questions to weed some applicants out, *you* want to end up presenting your skills. Rather than giving you answers to questions you may not be asked, it is more important to learn an *approach* to answering almost any interview question.

The Three Step Answer Formula

1. *Understand what is really being asked.*
   Most questions are really trying to find out about your self-management skills. While they are rarely this blunt, the employer's *real* question is often:
   - Can I depend on you?
   - Are you easy to get along with?
   - Are you a good worker?
   - Do you have the experience and training to do the job if we hire you?

2. *Answer the question briefly.*
   - Acknowledge the facts, but...
   - Present them as an advantage, not a disadvantage.
3. *Answer the real concern by presenting your related skills.*
   - Base your answer on your key skills (from the lists you did on pages 2-6).
   - Give examples to support your skills statements.

For example, if an employer says, "We were looking for someone with more experience in this field. Why should we consider you?"

Here is one possible answer: "I'm sure there are people who have more experience, but I *do* have over six years of work experience including three years of advanced training and hands-on experience using the latest methods and techniques. Because my training is recent, I am open to new ideas and am used to working hard and learning quickly."

Whatever your situation, learn to use it to your advantage! Use the three step process to practice your interview process. It works!

Dress and Grooming Rule

If you make a negative first impression, you won't get a second chance to make a good one. So do everything possible to make a good impression. A good rule for dressing for an interview is:

Dress like you think the boss will dress—only neater.

Dress for success! If necessary, get help selecting an interview outfit from someone who dresses well. Pay close attention to your grooming, too. Written things like correspondence and resumes must be neat and error-free since they create an impression as well.

Follow Up on All Contacts

People who follow up with potential employers and with others in their network get jobs faster than those who do not. Here are three rules:

1. *Send a thank you note to every person who helps you in your job search.*
2. *Send the thank you note within 24 hours after you speak with them.*
3. *Develop a system to follow up on "good" contacts.*

Thank You Notes

Thank you notes can be hand written or typed on nice paper and matching envelopes. Keep them simple, neat and error-free. Here's a sample:

2234 Riverwood Ave.
Philadelphia, PA 17963
April 16, 1992

Ms. Helen A. Colcord
Henderson & Associates, Inc.
1801 Washington Blvd., Suite 1201
Philadelphia, PA 17963

Dear Ms. Colcord:

Thank you for sharing your time with me so generously today. I really appreciate seeing your state-of-the-art computer equipment.

Your advice has already proved helpful. I have an appointment to meet with Mr. Robert Hopper on Friday. As you anticipated, he does intend to add more computer operators in the next few months.

In case you think of someone else who might need a person like me, I'm enclosing another JIST Card. I will let you know how the interview with Mr. Hopper goes.

Sincerely,

William Richardson

Job Lead Cards

Use a simple 3" x 5" card to keep essential information on each person in your network. Buy a 3" x 5" card file box and tabs for each day of the month. File the cards under the date you want to contact the person, and the rest is easy. I've found that staying in touch with a good contact every other week can pay off big. Here's a sample card to give you ideas to create your own:

Organization: Mutual Health Insurance
Contact Person: Anna Tomey   Phone: (317) 355-0216
Source of Lead: Aunt Ruth
Notes: 4/10-called. Anna on vacation. Call back 4/15. 4/15-Interview on 4/20 at 1:30. 4/20 Anna showed me around. They use the same computer we used in school! Friendly people. Sent thank you note & list card. Call back 5/1. 5/1-2nd interview on 5/8 at 9 am.

Essential Job Search Data

Complete this section in pencil to allow changes. Take it with you to help in completing applications. It will also help in answering interview questions and resume writing. In all sections, emphasize the skills and accomplishments that best support your ability to do the job you want! Use extra sheets as needed.

Key Accomplishments

List the three accomplishments which best prove your ability to do well in the kind of job you want.

1._____
2._____
3._____

Education/Training

Name of high school(s)/years attended:_____

_____

_____

Subjects related to job objective: _____

_____

_____

Extracurricular activities/hobbies/leisure activities: _____

_____

_____

Accomplishments/things you did well (in or out of school):_____

_____

_____

Schools you attended after high school, years attended, degrees/
certificates earned:_____

_____

_____

Courses related to job objective: _____

_____

_____

Extracurricular activities/hobbies/leisure activities: _____

_____

_____

Accomplishments/things you did well (in or out of school):_____

_____

_____

Military training, on-the-job or informal training, such as from a hobby, dates of training, type of certificate earned: _____

_____

_____

_____

_____

_____

Specific things you can do as a result: _____

_____

_____

_____

_____

_____

Work and Volunteer History

List your most recent job first, followed by each previous job. Include military experience and unpaid work here, too. Use additional sheets to cover *all* your significant jobs or unpaid experiences.

Whenever possible, provide numbers to support what you did: number of people served over one or more years, number of transactions processed, percent of sales increase, total inventory value you were responsible for, payroll of the staff you supervised, total budget you were responsible for, etc. As much as possible, mention results using numbers, too. These can be very impressive when mentioned in an interview or resume!

Job #1

Name of organization: _____

Address: _____

_____

Phone number: _____

Dates employed: _____

Job title(s): _____

Supervisor's name: _____

Details of any raises or promotions: _____

_____

_____

Machinery or equipment you handled: _____

_____

_____

Special skills this job required: _____

_____

_____

_____

List what you accomplished or did well:

_____

_____

_____

_____

Job # 2

Name of organization: _____

Address: _____

_____

Phone number: _____

Dates employed: _____

Job title(s): _____

Supervisor's name: _____

Details of any raises or promotions: _____

_____

_____

Machinery or equipment you handled: _____

_____

_____

Special skills this job required: _____

_____

_____

_____

List what did you accomplished or did well:

_____

_____

_____

_____

Job # 3

Name of organization: _____

Address: _____

_____

Phone number: _____

Dates employed: _____

Job title(s): _____

Supervisor's name: _____

Details of any raises or promotions: _____

_____

_____

Machinery or equipment you handled: _____

_____

_____

Special skills this job required: _____

_____

_____

_____

List what you accomplished or did well:

_____

_____

_____

_____

References

The best references are those who know your work *and* will say good things about you. This includes previous supervisors, teachers, coaches and others.

Contact your references and let them know what type of job you want and why you are qualified. Be sure to review what they will say about you! Since some employers will not give out references by phone or in person, have previous employers write a letter of reference for you in advance. If you have a bad reference from a previous employer, negotiate what they will say about you or get written references from other people you worked with there. When creating your list of references, be sure to include your reference's name and job title, where he or she works, their business address and phone number, how they know you, and what they will say about you.

Writing Your Resume

You have already learned that sending out resumes and waiting is *not* an effective job seeking technique. However, many employers *will* ask you for them, and they are a useful tool in your job search. Here are some basic tips to create a superior resume:

Write it yourself. It's OK to look at other resumes for ideas, but write yours yourself. It will force you to organize your thoughts and background.

Make it error free. One spelling or grammar error will create a negative impression. Get someone else to review your final draft for any errors. Then review it again!

Make it look good. Poor copy quality, cheap paper, bad type quality or anything else that creates a poor physical appearance will turn off employers to the best resume content. Get professional help with typing and printing if necessary. Most print shops can do it all for you.

Be brief, be relevant. Many good resumes fit on one page—few justify more than two. Include only the most important points. Use short sentences and action words. If it doesn't relate to and support the job objective, cut it!

Be honest. Don't overstate your qualifications. If you end up getting a job you can't handle, it will *not* be to your advantage. Most employers will see right through it and not hire you.

Be positive. Emphasize your accomplishments and results. This is no place to be too humble or to display your faults.

Be specific. Rather than "I am good with people." say "I supervised four people in the warehouse and increased productivity by 30 percent." Use numbers whenever possible, such as the number of people served, percent of increase, or dollar increase.

You should also know that everyone feels they are a resume expert. Whatever you do, someone will tell you it is wrong. For this reason, it is important to understand that a resume is a *job search tool.* You should *never* delay or slow down your job search because your resume is not "good enough." The best approach is to create a simple and acceptable resume as soon as possible, then use it! As time permits, make a better one if you feel you need to.

Simple Chronological Resume

This is the resume format most people use. It is a simple resume that presents previous experience in chronological order: the most recent experience is listed first followed by each previous job. Look at the resumes of Judith Jones on pages 28-29. Both are chronological resumes, but notice that the second resume includes some improvements over her first. The improved resume is clearly better, but both would be acceptable to most employers. Here are some tips for completing your basic resume:

Name: Use your formal name rather than a nickname if it sounds more professional.

Address: Be complete. Include zip code and avoid abbreviations. If you may move, use the address of a friend or relative or be certain to include a forwarding address.

Telephone Number: If your home number is often left unanswered during the day, include an alternate number where a message can be left. A reliable friend or relative will usually agree to this, but you could get an answering machine. Employers are

Simple Chronological Resume

Judith J. Jones   (317) 653-9217 (home)
115 South Hawthorne Avenue   (317) 272-7608 (leave message)
Chicago, Illinois 46204

JOB OBJECTIVE

Desire a position in the office management, secretarial or clerical area. Prefer a position requiring responsibility and a variety of tasks.

EDUCATION AND TRAINING

Acme Business College, Indianapolis, Indiana — Graduate of a one year business/secretarial program, 1982.

John Adams High School, South Bend, Indiana — Diploma, business education.

U.S. Army — Financial procedures, accounting functions.

Other: Continuing Education classes and workshops in business communication, scheduling systems, and customer relations.

EXPERIENCE

1981-1982 — Returned to school to complete and update my business skills. Learned word processing and other new office techniques.

1979-1981 — Claims Processor, Blue Spear Insurance Co., Indianapolis, Indiana. Handled customer medical claims, used a CRT, filed, miscellaneous clerical duties.

1978-1979 — Sales Clerk, Judy's Boutique, Indianapolis, Indiana. Responsible for counter sales, display design, and selected tasks.

1976-1978 — E4, U.S. Army. Assigned to various stations as a specialist in finance operations. Promoted prior to honorable discharge.

Previous jobs — Held part-time and summer jobs throughout high school.

PERSONAL

I am reliable, hard working, and good with people.

Improved Chronological Resume

Judith J. Jones   (317) 653-9217 (home)
115 South Hawthorne Avenue   (317) 272-7608 (message)
Chicago, Illinois 46204

POSITION DESIRED

Seeking position requiring excellent management and secretarial skills in office environment. Position could require a variety of tasks including typing, word processing, accounting/bookkeeping functions, and customer contact.

EDUCATION AND TRAINING

Acme Business College, Indianapolis, Indiana. Completed one year program in Professional Secretarial and Office Management. Grades in top 30% of my class. Courses: word processing, accounting theory and systems, time management, basic supervision & others.

John Adams High School, South Bend, Indiana. Graduated with emphasis on business and secretarial courses. Won shorthand contest.

Other: Continuing education at my own expense (Business Communications, Customer Relations, Computer Applications, other courses).

EXPERIENCE

1981-1982 — Returned to Business School to update skills. Advanced coursework in accounting and office management. Learned to operate word processing equipment including Wang, IBM, DEC. Gained operating knowledge of computers.

1979-1981 — Claims Processor, Blue Spear Insurance Company, Indianapolis, Indiana. Handled 50 complex medical insurance claims per day — 18% above department average. Received two merit raises for performance.

1978-1979 — Assistant Manager, Judy's Boutique, Indianapolis, Indiana. Managed sales, financial records, inventory, purchasing, correspondence and related tasks during owner's absence. Supervised four employees. Sales increased 15% during my tenure.

1976-1978 — Finance Specialist (E4), U.S. Army. Responsible for the systematic processing of 500 invoices per day from commercial vendors. Trained and supervised eight others. Devised internal system allowing 15% increase in invoices processed with a decrease in personnel.

1972-1976 — Various part-time and summer jobs through high school. Learned to deal with customers, meet deadlines and other skills.

SPECIAL SKILLS AND ABILITIES

80 words per minute on electric typewriter, more on word processor, can operate most office equipment. Good math skills. Accept supervision, able to supervise others. Excellent attendance record.

PERSONAL

I have excellent references, learn quickly, and am willing to relocate.

most likely to try to reach you by phone, so having a reliable way to be reached is very important.

Job Objective: This is optional for a very basic resume but is still important to include. Notice that Judy is keeping her options open with her objective. Saying "Secretary" or "Clerical" might limit her to lower paying jobs, or even prevent her from being considered for jobs she might take.

Education and Training: Include any formal training you've had plus any training that supports the job you seek. If you did not finish a formal degree or program, list what you did complete. Include any special accomplishments.

Previous Experience: The standard approach is to list employer, job title, dates employed and responsibilities. But there are better ways of presenting your experience. Look over the "Improved Chronological Resume" for ideas. The improved version emphasizes results, accomplishments and performance.

Personal Data: Neither of the sample resumes have the standard height, weight, marital status included on so many resumes. That information is simply not relevant! If you do include some personal information, put it at the bottom and keep it related to the job you want.

References: There is no need to list references. If employers want them, they will ask. If your references are particularly good, it's OK to say so.

Improved Chronological Resume

Once you have a simple, error-free and eye-pleasing resume, get on with your job search. There is no reason to delay! But you may want to create a better one in your spare time evenings and/or weekends. If you do, here are some tips:

Job Objective: Job titles often limit the type of jobs for which you will be considered. Instead, think of the type of work you want to do and can do well and describe it in more general terms. Instead of "Restaurant Manager," for example, say "Managing a small to mid-sized business" if that is what you are qualified to do.

Education and Training: New graduates should emphasize their recent training and education more than those with five years or so of recent and related work experience. Think about any special accomplishments while in school and include these if they relate to the job. Did you work full time while in school? Did you do particularly well in work-related classes, get an award, participate in sports?

Skills and Accomplishments: Employers are interested in what you accomplished and did well. Include those things that relate to doing well in the job you are after now. Even "small" things count. Perhaps your attendance was perfect, you met a tight deadline, did the work of others during vacations, etc. Be specific and include numbers—even if you have to estimate them.

Job Titles: Many job titles don't accurately reflect the job you did. For example, your job title may have been "cashier" but you also opened the store, trained new staff, and covered for the boss on vacations. Perhaps "Head Cashier and Assistant Manager" would be more accurate. Check with your previous employer if not sure.

Promotions: If you were promoted or got good evaluations, say so. A promotion to a more responsible job can be handled as a separate job if this makes sense.

Problem Areas: Employers look for any sign of instability or lack of reliability. It is very expensive to hire and train someone who won't stay or who won't work out. Gaps in employment, jobs held for short periods of time or a lack of direction in the jobs you've held are all things that employers are concerned about. If you have any legitimate explanation, use it. For example:

"1987—Continued my education at..."
"1988—Traveled extensively throughout the U.S."
"1988 to present—Self-employed barn painter and widget maker"
"1989—Had first child, took year off before returning to work"

Use entire years or even seasons of years to avoid displaying a shorter gap you can't explain easily: "Spring 1988—Fall 1989" will not show you as unemployed from January to March, 1988, for example.

Remember that a resume can get you screened out, but it is up to you to get the interview and the job. So, cut out *anything* that is negative in your resume!

Skills Resume

ALAN ATWOOD
3231 East Harbor Road
Grand Rapids, Michigan 41103
Home: (303) 447-2111   Message (303) 547-8201

Objective: A responsible position in retail sales

Areas of Accomplishment:

Customer Service	• Communicate well with all age groups. • Able to interpret customer concerns to help them find the items they want. • Received 6 Employee of the Month awards in 3 years.
Merchandise Display	• Developed display skills via in-house training and experience. • Received Outstanding Trainee Award for Christmas Toy Display. • Dress mannequins, arrange table displays, and organize sale merchandise.
Stock Control and Marketing	• Maintained and marked stock during department manager's 6 week illness. • Developed more efficient record-keeping procedures.
Additional Skills	• Operate cash register, IBM compatible hardware, calculators, and electronic typewriters. • Punctual, honest, reliable, and a hard-working self-starter.
Experience:	Harper's Department Store Grand Rapids, Michigan 1984 to Present
Education:	Central High School Grand Rapids, Michigan 3.6/4.0 grade point average Honor Graduate in Distributive Education Two years retail sales training in Distributive Education. Also courses in Business Writing, Accounting, Typing, and Word Processing.

Skills Resume

LILI LI LU
1536 Sierra Way • Piedmont, California 97435 • Telephone 436-3874

OBJECTIVE
Program Development, Coordination & Administration
Especially in a people-oriented organization where there is a need to assure broad cooperation through the use of sound planning and strong administration and persuasive skills to achieve community goals.

MAJOR AREAS OF EXPERTISE AND ABILITY
Budgeting & Management for Sound Program Development
With partner, established new association devoted to maximum personal development and self-realization for each of its members. Over a period of time, administered budget totaling $285,000. Jointly planned growth of group and related expenditures, investments, programs, and development of property holdings to realize current and long-term goals. As a result, holdings increased 25 fold over the period, reserves invested increased 1200%, and all major goals for members have been achieved.

Purchasing to Assure Smooth Flow of Needed Supplies and Services
Made most purchasing decisions to assure maximum production from available funds. Maintained continuous stock inventory to meet on-going needs, selected suppliers, assured proper disbursements to achieve a strong continuing line of credit while minimizing financing costs.

Transportation Management
Determined transportation needs of group. Assured maximum utilization of limited motor pool. Arranged four major moves of all facilities, furnishings, and equipment to new locations — two across country.

Other Functions Performed
Crisis management, proposal preparation, political analysis, nutrition, recreation planning and administration, stock market operations, taxes, community organization, social affairs administration (including VIP entertaining), landscaping (two awards for excellence), contract negotiations, teaching and more.

SOME SPECIFIC RESULTS
Above experience gained in 20 years devoted to family development and household management in partnership with my husband, Harvy Wangchung Lu, who is equally responsible for results produced. **Primary achievements:** Son Lee, 19, honor student at Harvard majoring in physics, state forensics champion. Daughter Su, 18, leading candidate for U.S. Olympic team in gymnastics, entering pre-law studies at the U of C, Berkeley. **Secondary achievements:** President of Piedmont High School PTA two years. Organized successful citizen protest to stop incursion of Oakland commercialism on Piedmont area. Appointed by Robert F. Kennedy as coordinator of his campaign in Oakland.

PERSONAL DATA AND OTHER FACTS
Bachelor of Arts (Asian History), Cody College, Cody, California. Highly active in community affairs. Have learned that there is a spark of genius in almost everyone, which, when nurtured, can flare into dramatic achievement.

(adapted from *Who's Hiring Who?* by Richard Lathrop, Ten Speed Press, 1987.)

Did you guess that Lili is a homemaker?

The Combination Resume

Thomas Welborn

637 Wickham Road
Phoenix, AZ 85009

Home: (602) 253-9678
Leave Message: (602) 257-6643

JOB OBJECTIVE

Position in the electronics industry requiring skills in the design, sale, installation, maintenance, and repair of audio, video, and other advanced electronics. Prefer tasks needing creative problem-solving skills and customer contact.

EDUCATION

ITT TECHNICAL INSTITUTE

Phoenix, AZ
A.S. Degree,
Electronics Engineering
Technology
1987-present

Completed a comprehensive, two-year curriculum including over 2000 hours of class and advanced laboratory. Theoretical, practical and hands-on knowledge of audio and RF amplifiers, AM/FM transmitter-receiver cirucits, OP amplifiers, microwave and radar communications, digital circuits, and much more. Excellent attendance while working part time to pay tuition. Graduating in top 25%.

PLAINS JR. COLLEGE

Phoenix, AZ

Courses included digital electronics, programming, business, and 1986 computer applications. Worked full time and maintained a B+ average.

DESERT VIEW H.S.

1984 graduate

College prep. courses including advanced math, business, marketing, merchandising, computer orientation, and Basic programming. Very active in varsity sports. National Jr. Honor Society for two years.

page one

The Combination Resume

SKILLS

PROBLEM-SOLVING: Familiar with the underlying theory of most electronic systems and am particularly strong in isolating problems by using logic and persistence. I enjoy the challenge of solving complex problems and will work long hours, if necessary, to do this on a deadline.

INTERPERSONAL: Have supervised five staff and trained many more. Comfortable with one-to-one and small group communications. Can explain technical issues simply to customers of varying levels of sophistication. Had over 10,000 customer contacts in one job with no complaints and several written commendations.

TECHNICAL: Background in a variety of technical areas including medical equipment, consumer electronics, computers, automated cash registers, photocopiers, standard office and computer equipment and peripherals. Have designed special application combinational and sequential logic circuits using TTL logic. Constructed Z-80 microprocessor and wrote several machine language programs for this system. Can diagnose and repair problems in digital and analog circuits.

ORGANIZATIONAL: Have set up and run my own small business and worked in another responsible job while going to school full time. Earned enough money to live independently and pay all school expenses during this time. I can work independently and have learned to use my time efficiently.

EXPERIENCE

BANDLER'S INN: 1984-present. Waiter, promoted to night manager. Complete responsibility for all operations of a shift grossing over $300,000 in sales per year. Supervised five full-time and three part-time staff. Business increased during my employment by 35% and profits by 42%, much of it due to word of mouth advertising of satisfied customers.

FRANKLIN HOSPITAL: 1983-84. Electronic Service Technicians's Assistant. Worked in Medical, Physics, and Electronics Departments. Assisted technicians in routine service and maintenance of a variety of hospital equipment. Part time while going to school.

TOM'S YARD SERVICE: 1981-1985. Set up a small business while in school. Worked part-time and summers doing yard work. Made enough money to buy a car and save for tuition.

Skills and Combination Resumes

There are no firm rules on how you should do your resume. Different formats make sense for different people.

Besides the chronological format, the functional or "skills" resume is often used. This resume emphasizes your most important *skills*, supported by specific examples of how you have used them. This approach allows you to use any part of your life history to support your ability to do the job you want.

While the skills resume can be very effective, it does require more work to create. And some employers don't like them because they can hide a job seeker's faults better than a chronological resume (such as job gaps, lack of formal education or no related work experience).

Still, a skills resume may make sense for you. Look over the sample resumes on pages 32-35 for ideas. Notice that the resume on pages 34-35 includes elements of a skills *and* a chronological resume. These are called "combination" resumes — an approach that makes sense if your previous job history or education and training is a positive.

The Quick Job Search Review

Go at your job search as if it were a job itself. Get organized and spend at least 25 hours per week actively looking. Follow up on all the leads you generate and send thank you notes. If you want to get a good job quickly, you must get lots of interviews!

Pay attention to all the details, then be yourself in the interview. Remember that employers are people, too. They will hire someone they feel will do the job well, who will be reliable, and who will fit easily into their work environment. When you want the job, tell the employer why they should hire you. Tell them you want the job and why. It's that simple.

I wish you well in your job search and your life.